THE

MILLIONAIRE

BASICS

**Your Sure Companion For
Achieving Financial Success in the
21st Century**

Dr. Brian Ialeen

Table of contents

Introduction

Your actions have a much larger impact on your financial success than your level of information. Even highly intelligent people may find it difficult to alter their behavior. Investing, personal finance, and business decisions are typically framed as quantitative fields that use data and formulae to recommend specific actions. But this theoretical model doesn't match up with reality because people don't make financial decisions based on numbers alone. Instead, they negotiate these decisions over a meal or in a conference, when factors such as individual histories and perspectives, group dynamics, marketing strategies, and unconventional incentives all come into play.

I hope you find something in this book to enjoy, so I'll try not to make too many references to myself. Let me tell you about Jerusha, a friend of mine.

Where Jerusha and I grew up, most of the young women in town were successful entrepreneurs. We were both young women, yeah, but not particularly successful ones. My family couldn't afford education for me, but she got a leg up because hers were average. She was intelligent and self-motivated, with the same goal of becoming a doctor as her mother had. Jerusha's passion for making a difference in the field of medicine was ignited at a young age, and her fascination with the human body's inner workings began at an early age.

Tragically, her parents were killed in an automobile accident on the way home from dropping off the tuition payment. That was the first stop on Jerusha's adventure. Her parents were on their way to pay her tuition to one of the best medical schools in the country when they passed away. She continued on anyway, using the loss of her parents as inspiration. She went away to college, and I haven't seen her since. Things didn't always go swimmingly for her. She worked two jobs and devoted countless hours to her studies in order to put herself through medical school. Her days consisted of endless lectures and clinical rotations, and her nights were spent awake studying.

Jerusha, despite facing increasing opposition, steadfastly pursued her goals. Her dedication to medicine was her north star. She was driven by her ambition to make a positive difference in people's lives through healthcare. Jerusha endured years of rigorous coursework and several exams before passing out of medical school with honours. Student loan debt was hanging over her head like a black cloud. Jerusha began her residency unfazed, working long hours and putting her own life on hold to care for her patients.

Jerusha's life took a surprising turn during her residency.   While caring for a seriously ill patient one night, she crossed paths with Daniel, a prosperous businessman. Daniel approached Jerusha after being moved by her kindness and persistence and soon learnt of her financial struggles.

Daniel was moved by her narrative and inspired by her tenacity, so he offered to be her business coach. He educated Jerusha on the nuances of the business world, including investing, starting a company, and making a budget. The learning curve was extremely steep, and Jerusha frequently felt overwhelmed.

Jerusha balanced the rigours of residency with her newfound interest in promoting financial literacy for a whole two years. She learned everything she could by reading, going to seminars, and consulting with professionals. Despite encountering obstacles and experiencing periods of doubt, she remained steadfast in the pursuit of her goal.

Then, on the 23rd of March, everything she had worked for finally started to pay off. She made her first investment, and it turned out to be quite lucrative. Jerusha's financial savvy improved over the next months, and she began making more calculated investments. When she started making more money, she put it toward her debt.

Jerusha's investment portfolio grew steadily over the years, and she developed a keen eye for the stock market. Her career in medicine flourished, and she gained widespread acclaim as a result. Jerusha's hard work and increased knowledge in finance helped her earn her first million.

However, Jerusha's voyage was not just about the money; it was also a demonstration of the value of persistence and unyielding will. Not only did she realize her ambition of becoming a prominent physician, but she also excelled in the business sector. Many were motivated by Jerusha's narrative, which demonstrated that any obstacle could be surmounted with hard work, the appropriate mindset about money, and perseverance.

The question arises, how do I know all these? It was her! In a word, yes. Three months ago, after all this time, she finally contacted and requested to meet up. We had a lot to discuss now that we were both billionaires. After we confided in one other about our trials and tribulations, I found the strength to put together this book.

Less ego, more riches is the theme of a couple quotes I'd like to leave you with before I go more into this finding;

- You shouldn't base your financial decisions on the strategies of those who aren't in the same game as you.
- If you're good at investing, then patience should be your secret weapon. This is the crux of the compounding process.

- People's ability to save money is under their control more than they assume.
- Until you're the one actually doing the work, everything appears simple.
- The two concepts of chance and danger are related.
- From the outside looking in, successful investment may appear easy, but it is tremendously difficult to keep a long-term perspective during stock market downturns.
- Getting money is easy, but keeping it is much trickier.
- When you really want something to be true, you tend to believe stories that exaggerate how likely it is.
- The value of money depends on what you need it for.
- When one's income rises above a specific threshold, one can be classified as a saver, someone who thinks they can't save, or someone

who doesn't think they need to save.

- More so than flaunting wealth, demonstrating humility, kindness, and empathy can win you respect.
- While it's important to have a strategy, the most important part of any plan is being prepared for things to not go as planned.
- It's not the same thing to become affluent as it is to remain wealthy.
- It's easy to discount non-monetary aspects of price until you have to deal with them in the heat of the moment.
- The highest returns aren't always the best way to invest, especially since they're typically flukes. It's all about generating stable profits over the long term so that compound interest can do its thing.
- The compounding effect means that the impact of tail occurrences is frequently underappreciated. The events of September 11 had far-

reaching repercussions, including as the housing bubble and the subsequent financial crisis.

- Increasing your investing horizon is the single most effective way to boost your returns.
- Making money versus keeping it.
- His expertise is in the financial markets, but his true weapon is time. That is the process of compounding in action.

Being financially successful depends on more than just our wits; our actions also play a significant role. Even for exceptionally bright people, it can be difficult to instil good financial habits. However, regular individuals who lack formal financial education might still amass riches by developing certain behavioural talents that have nothing to do with traditional intelligence tests.

It's vital to remember that each person is one of a kind, with their own quirks, experiences, and aspirations. Thus, we have varying levels of comfort with financial risk and perspectives on saving and investing. People who experienced the Great Depression may evaluate risk and reward differently than those who were born and raised during a time of low inflation and low interest rates.

Quantitative components of finance, such as building a diversified portfolio of low-cost index funds, are rather simple to grasp. This book does not encourage readers to take on the intimidating stock market in an attempt to get superior results. Instead, it emphasises the more difficult task of understanding human behaviour and the decisions we make in order to maintain a healthy work-life balance and appropriate stock market returns. However, learning about human behavior is accessible and interesting for everybody, regardless of their background or expertise.

Take nothing anyone says about you personally. As humans, we have to deal with a wide range of difficulties and, on occasion, unpleasant surprises. How we respond is the only thing that counts. Challenges of any size can be reduced to insignificance by the use of our gathered wisdom.

The way we react to the unexpected death of a loved one, the flooding of our home from a burst pipe, or the collapse of the stock market is essentially the same every time. We can either blame the stock market, our broker, or Wall Street for investment losses, leading to a lonely and resentful existence, or we can blame doctors, hospitals, and isolation from friends and family. For instance, many investors had a prolonged negative reaction after the 2008 financial crisis, meaning they missed out on the historic bull market. It's how we react that matters, not what happens to us. This book can help disheartened investors find their footing so they can confidently re-enter the market.

Disregard the opinions of others.

Achieving financial success is not solely determined by our level of intelligence, but rather it is greatly influenced by our behaviour and actions. Educating individuals on effective financial behaviour can pose challenges, even for those who possess high levels of intelligence. It is important to understand that even individuals with exceptional intelligence can experience financial difficulties if they struggle to manage their emotions. On the other hand, individuals without formal financial education but possessing certain behavioural skills, unrelated to traditional measures of intelligence, can still amass wealth.

It is important to recognize and understand that each individual possesses their own distinct set of characteristics, including their personality traits, upbringing, educational background, and aspirations. As a result, it is important to recognize that our individual risk tolerance and attitudes towards money, saving, and investing can vary. For example, it is important to note that individuals who experienced the Great Depression may possess distinct perspectives on the concepts of risk and reward when compared to millennials who have grown up in a time characterized by low inflation and low interest rates.

One of the key components in finance is comprehending the quantitative aspects, which involves various elements such as constructing a diversified portfolio of low-cost index funds. This particular aspect can be considered relatively straightforward in comparison to other concepts in finance. This book aims to educate individuals about the stock market without promoting the idea of competing against it to achieve above-average returns. Instead, the primary focus lies in understanding our behavior and the decisions we make in order to maintain a well-rounded lifestyle while also attaining satisfactory returns in the stock market. This particular aspect tends to be more demanding and requires careful consideration.

However, it is important to note that comprehending our behaviour is both attainable and captivating, irrespective of your current abilities, background, or understanding. Throughout our journey in life, we often encounter a multitude of challenges and occasionally find ourselves confronted with unwelcome surprises. What is truly important is our response or reaction to different situations. Making wise decisions based on the knowledge and lessons we have gained throughout our lives can help us overcome even the most daunting challenges, ultimately making them seem less significant in the grand scheme of things.

The way we react to different situations, such as the unexpected death of a loved one, damage to our home caused by a broken water pipe, or a significant decline in the stock market, is essentially similar. One option we have is to attribute responsibility to doctors and hospitals, which may result in us feeling isolated from our loved ones and harboring negative emotions. Alternatively, we can choose to place blame on the stock market, our broker, or Wall Street for any financial losses we may have experienced. Many investors experienced negative reactions for a prolonged period of time, resulting in missed opportunities during the historic bull market. This was primarily due to the losses they incurred as a result of the 2008 financial crisis. Regardless of our level of experience, it is important to consider how we choose to respond in any given situation. This book has the potential to provide valuable guidance to investors who have experienced unfortunate circumstances, helping them regain their emotional stability and reestablish their confidence when reentering the market.

Chapter 1:Overview of the psychology of money

The field of study known as the psychology of money is both fascinating and complex. It explores the intricate ways in which individuals think, feel, and behave in relation to money. Money serves as a valuable tool for facilitating economic transactions, allowing individuals to exchange goods and services. However, it is important to recognize that money holds a deeper psychological significance that goes beyond its practical purpose. In this overview, we will delve into the fundamental aspects of the psychology of money, aiming to educate and shed light on its significance in various areas such as personal finance, relationships, and overall well-being.

In understanding the Psychological Impact of Finances In today's society, money plays a significant role in our lives. It not only serves as a means of exchange but also carries a substantial emotional weight. The way we perceive and handle our finances can have a profoundOne key element in understanding the psychology of money is the emotional connection that individuals often develop towards it. Money has the ability to elicit various emotions within individuals. These emotions can span from feelings of happiness and a sense of safety when one possesses an abundance of money, to feelings of unease and tension when confronted with financial challenges. An illustration of this concept is that when an individual receives a raise at their place of employment, it can evoke a sense of achievement and contentment. Conversely, when unexpected medical expenses arise, it can elicit feelings of unease and concern.

- The Role of Childhood and Upbringing: Childhood and upbringing play a crucial role in shaping an individual's development and future outcomes. The experiences and environment during these formative years have a profound impact on various aspects of a person's life, including their cognitive, emotional, and social development. DuringDuring our formative years, a significant influence on our attitudes and behaviours towards money is observed. An example of how a person's upbringing can influence their financial habits is when they grow up in a family that prioritises frugality. In such a household, the individual may be more likely to develop a keen interest in saving money and making wise investment decisions.
- Money Mindsets: It is important to understand that individuals often

possess certain money mindsets that can significantly impact the way they make financial choices. Mindsets have the potential to either empower individuals or impose limitations on them. Here are some examples:

The scarcity mindset refers to a belief system where individuals perceive that there is a perpetual lack of financial resources, which often leads to feelings of fear and a tendency to accumulate and hold onto money.Having a limiting mindset can hinder our growth and potential. It is important to recognize when we are holding ourselves back with negative beliefs or self

The abundance mindset refers to the ability to recognize and embrace opportunities for financial growth while maintaining an open and receptive attitude towards abundance.Developing an empowering mindset is crucial for personal growth and success. It involves cultivating a positive and confident outlook on life, which allows you

The Safety-First Mindset refers to the practice of giving utmost importance to financial security and adopting measures to minimize risks in all circumstances.Having a limiting mindset can hinder personal growth and success. It is important to recognize and challenge any negative beliefs or thoughts that may be holding

YOLO, an acronym for "You Only Live Once," is a popular phrase often used to emphasise the importance of seizing opportunities and living life to the fullest. It serves as a reminder that life is finite and should be cherished. Mindset: It is important to understand the potential consequences of prioritising immediate pleasures over long-term planning.

Understanding the Influence of Emotions on Financial DecisionsIt is important to understand that emotions can greatly influence our spending habits. In certain situations, such as following a particularly demanding day, individuals may resort to a practice known as "retail therapy" as a means to temporarily alleviate stress, despite the potential negative impact it may have on their financial well-being. Similarly, it is important to note that receiving a windfall, such as winning the lottery, can sometimes result in impulsive spending driven by the exhilaration of suddenly acquiring a significant amount of money.

- Financial stress is a common concern that can have a significant impact on one's mental well-being. Constantly worrying about money, accumulating debts, and facing an uncertain financial future can potentially contribute to the development of conditions such as anxiety and depression. It is important to note that various studies have indicated that financial stress can have a significant impact on an individual's mental well-being, comparable to the effects of other stressors in life.

- Money and Relationships: It is important to understand that money can have a significant impact on personal relationships. It is important to note that disagreements regarding finances often arise as a common source of conflict among partners. In some cases, it is common for couples to have different priorities when it comes to financial planning. For example, one partner may place a higher importance on saving money for the future, while the other partner may have a preference for enjoying the present and spending money on immediate pleasures. In order to foster strong and positive financial relationships, it is crucial to prioritize effective communication and develop a deep understanding of one another's money beliefs and values.

Behavioural economics is a field of study that combines insights from psychology and economics to understand how individuals make decisions about money. It explores the ways in which our behaviour and cognitive biases can influence our financial choices. Money playsBehavioral economics is a fascinating field that delves into the ways in which our cognitive biases can impact the choices we make when it comes to our finances. By studying these biases, researchers are able to gain a deeper understanding of why we sometimes make irrational or suboptimal decisions in the realm of money management. This knowledge can be incredibly valuable in helping individuals and organisations make more informed and rational financial choices. **One interesting cognitive bias that affects individuals is known as "loss aversion."** This bias refers to the tendency of people to have a stronger inclination to avoid losses compared to acquiring equivalent gains. As a consequence, this bias can lead to making suboptimal financial decisions, such as holding onto investments that are experiencing losses.

- The Pursuit of Happiness and Fulfilment: Although money can offer comfort and security, it is important to understand that it alone does not guarantee happiness. The field of psychology recognizes that our well-being is shaped by a multitude of factors, such as our relationships with others, our personal development, and the experiences we go through. This understanding highlights the interconnectedness between these different aspects and how they contribute to our overall happiness and fulfilment. Achieving overall happiness requires finding a harmonious equilibrium between financial goals and non-material sources of fulfilment.

It is crucial to have a grasp on the psychology of money in order to make well-informed financial decisions, strengthen relationships, and enhance mental well-being. The field of study being discussed here is known for its ability to provide valuable insights into the reasons behind people's behaviours when it comes to money. Additionally, it offers various strategies that can be employed to attain both financial success and a sense of fulfilment in life. In the course of this book, we will embark on a comprehensive exploration of these subjects and examine practical strategies for effectively utilising the principles of psychology in relation to money, ultimately leading to personal advantages.

Chapter:2 Importance of understanding money psychology

Gaining a deep comprehension of the psychology behind money is crucial in the modern world, as our financial choices play a significant role in nearly every facet of our lives. The comprehension of this concept extends beyond mere knowledge of earning and managing money. It explores the intricate connection between individuals and their financial resources. In this discussion, we will delve into the importance of understanding money psychology, supported by various examples and illustrations.

- **Understanding the Importance of Making Informed Financial Decisions**:Understanding the psychological factors that influence our money choices is crucial for making well-informed financial decisions. Let's take the case of an individual who possesses awareness about their inclination towards impulsive spending during periods of stress. With this valuable knowledge at their disposal, individuals can acquire the necessary tools to effectively manage stress-induced spending. By implementing strategic approaches, they can safeguard their financial well-being in the long run.

- Overcoming Limiting Beliefs: It is important to understand that many individuals may hold certain beliefs about money that can restrict their financial growth. These beliefs, often referred to as limiting money beliefs, can act as barriers to achieving financial success. To overcome these beliefs, it is crucial to first gain a comprehensive understanding of their origins. For example, when an individual holds the belief that they will never attain wealth because of their upbringing, it is important to acknowledge that this belief has been shaped by their childhood experiences. By understanding this connection, they can gain the knowledge and confidence needed to question and transform this belief.

- Financial resilience: is an essential aspect to consider in today's unpredictable world. Understanding the psychological aspects of managing financial setbacks can be beneficial for individuals in overcoming challenges and recovering from difficult situations. During periods of economic decline, it is important to have knowledge about the psychology of fear and the inclination to hastily sell investments. This understanding can help individuals make informed decisions and avoid impulsive actions that may result in significant financial losses.

- **Enhancing Financial Communication:** Gaining insight into the psychology of money can greatly benefit relationships. Couples who engage in open and honest conversations about their money values, goals, and emotions tend to have a higher likelihood of effectively managing and resolving financial conflicts. An example of this is when one partner has a tendency to overspend when they feel deprived. By being aware of this, the other partner can approach the conversation with empathy and focus on finding constructive solutions.

- Investing wisely requires careful consideration as there are numerous psychological pitfalls that can influence investment decisions. Understanding and being aware of common biases, such as overconfidence or herd behaviour, can help individuals make more rational and informed investment decisions. An investor who is knowledgeable about the concept of "herd mentality" may choose to avoid the temptation of blindly following the crowd during periods of market euphoria. By doing so, they can protect themselves from potential losses that may occur during a subsequent downturn.
- Financial Happiness and Fulfilment: It is commonly believed that pursuing financial goals can contribute to one's overall happiness and fulfillment in life. By recognizing that happiness can be

affected by both material possessions and non-material aspects, individuals are empowered to find a harmonious equilibrium. It is important to understand that an individual who is solely focused on amassing wealth may unintentionally overlook the immense value that experiences and relationships can bring to their overall well-being.

- Understanding Money Psychology for Effective Financial Policies: Governments and institutions can enhance their ability to design effective economic policies by gaining a comprehensive understanding of money psychology. One example of understanding human behavior is acknowledging that individuals often delay saving for retirement. This awareness can prompt the introduction of automatic savings programs, which can assist individuals in safeguarding their financial future.

- Personal Growth and Self-Awareness: By delving into the realm of money psychology, individuals have the opportunity to embark on a journey of personal growth and enhance their self-awareness. This prompts individuals to engage in introspection, encouraging them to contemplate their personal values, priorities, and aspirations for the future. An instance could be when an individual realizes that their relentless pursuit of wealth is primarily motivated by a desire for social standing. This realization prompts them to reevaluate the overall meaning and direction of their life, ultimately allowing them to redefine success based on their own personal values and aspirations.

Gaining knowledge about the psychology of money can be compared to having a valuable tool that guides us through the complex landscape of personal finance and human behaviour. By acquiring knowledge and understanding about personal finance, individuals are equipped with the necessary tools to manage their money effectively. This not only helps them improve their financial well-being but also strengthens their relationships with others. When individuals have a solid grasp of financial concepts, they can communicate more effectively with their partners, family members, and friends about money matters. This open dialogue fosters trust, transparency, and cooperation, ultimately leading to stronger relationships. Additionally, education in personal finance cultivates resilience in individuals. It equips them with the skills to navigate financial challenges and setbacks, enabling them to bounce back and recover more quickly. By developing financial literacy, individuals are better prepared to handle unexpected expenses, emergencies, or economic downturns. Ultimately, the knowledge gained through financial education contributes to a more fulfilled and balanced life. It empowers individuals to take control of their financial future, make In the pages of this book, we will embark on a journey to explore these concepts in greater detail. Our aim is to provide you with valuable knowledge and effective strategies that can help you leverage the fascinating field of money psychology to your advantage.

Chapter 3: Historical Perspectives on Money

In order to gain a comprehensive understanding of the psychology of money, it is imperative that we embark on an exploration of its historical development and the significant influence it has exerted on human behaviour and society as a whole. The exploration of money's history is crucial in order to fully understand how it became intricately connected with our emotions, beliefs, and attitudes. In this lesson, we will embark on a historical exploration, examining the evolution of currency and its initial psychological significance.

Throughout the course of human civilization, money has played a significant role in our society. It has taken on various forms and has been an integral part of our daily lives for thousands of years. In the beginning, barter systems were dependent on the exchange of goods and services; however, it is important to note that these systems did have certain limitations. The introduction of money as a medium of exchange brought about a significant revolution in the realms of trade and commerce. In ancient cultures, the utilisation of shells as a form of currency provided a means for conducting transactions that were both more efficient and adaptable.

The psychological impact of early exposure to money is a topic of great interest and importance. It is crucial to understand how the presence of money in a child's life from an early age can shape their attitudes, beliefs, and behaviours related to finances. The adoption of money has indeed brought about significant changes in human behaviour. The concepts of ownership, wealth accumulation, and the pursuit of material possessions were fostered. Individuals started assigning significance to various forms of metal or paper, consequently impacting their perception of safety and personal value. Ancient civilizations, such as the Egyptians and Greeks, utilised coins not solely for the purpose of trade, but also as significant representations of power and status.

In regards to cultural and societal influences, it is important to note that the psychological significance of money can differ among various cultures and societies. Throughout history, various societies have placed different levels of importance on money, which can be seen as a reflection of their distinct belief systems and priorities. In certain cultures, the accumulation of wealth is regarded as an indication of both success and virtue. Conversely, in other cultures, spiritual or communal values are prioritised over the pursuit of material gain.

Lets discuss early psychological theories. These theories were developed by pioneering psychologists who laid the foundation for the field of psychology as we know it today. It is in the early stages of psychological theories, there was also an exploration of the connection between money and human behaviour. One example of a scholar who explored the notion of "money neuroses" is Sigmund Freud. In his work, Freud delved into the idea that money can serve as a representation of underlying psychological conflicts and desires. The work that he conducted established the fundamental basis for comprehending the emotional aspects that underlie issues pertaining to money.

In this discussion, we will be exploring the fascinating period known as the Gold Standard Era. The gold standard, which refers to a monetary system in which a nation's currency is supported by a fixed quantity of gold, had a significant and far-reaching psychological influence. The monetary system was able to instil trust among individuals, leading them to have a sense of confidence in the value of their money. The abandonment of the gold standard in the 20th century brought about a significant change in the way people perceive money, as the connection between tangible assets and currency became less evident.

In regards to the topic of modern currency and digital money, it is important to note that the introduction of modern currency, which includes paper bills and coins, has played a significant role in distancing money from physical assets. In recent decades, we have witnessed the emergence of digital money and cryptocurrencies, which have introduced a novel dimension to our understanding of the psychology of money. The concept of digital currencies, such as Bitcoin, presents a unique challenge to our traditional understanding of money due to their intangibility.To truly grasp the historical perspectives on money, it is crucial to recognize that it has consistently held a significance that extends beyond its role as a mere medium of exchange. Throughout the course of human history, money has played a pivotal role in shaping societies, exerting influence over individual behaviors, and carrying significant symbolic and psychological weight. Understanding the historical context is of utmost importance in order to fully grasp the significance of money and its enduring prominence in our lives. It is imperative to delve into the psychology of money, as it is a subject that warrants exploration and comprehension in our modern era.

3 i : Evolution of money and its impact on human behaviour

Money has always been important and has shaped communities. Its varied manifestations have shaped human behaviour for aeons. By studying the evolution of barter systems to modern currencies, we can better grasp how money affects our psychology and behaviour.

Today,we'll review the fascinating barter system and its limits. You may know that barter is an ancient technique of exchanging products and services without money. It was vital to early human societies and widely used.

In early human culture, barter was the main form of trade. In the past, people traded products and services based on the "double coincidence of wants." This indicates that both sides must want what the other is offering. However, barter systems had drawbacks. One restriction was the need for perfect product matches. This meant people had to find someone with the thing they wanted and have an item the other person wanted in return. Barter systems also have value storage issues. Unlike current currency, bartered goods were difficult to store and maintain.

The historical development of commodity money is based on the intrinsic worth of a physical item.

To overcome barter's drawbacks, cultures adopted commodities with inherent value to facilitate commerce. Early human civilization used crops, cattle, and precious metals like gold and silver as currency. The switch to commodity money, my dear pupil, was a major economic development. As people collected these goods, the idea of acquiring wealth emerged.

Standardised coins in ancient civilizations like the Greeks and Romans had a profound psychological impact. Coins have always symbolised power, authority, and prosperity. Having a lot of coinage was not only useful, but it also showed status and social standing. My dear pupil, standardised currency began a psychological link between money and identity.

The shift from commodity to paper money changed how people viewed and used money. To understand paper money, you must realise that its value depends on trust in the issuer. This can be a bank or government. The trust in the paper note changed human behaviour and perception. Individuals must trust the trustworthiness and ethics of the organisations that support and govern money in order to traverse the current financial world.

we'll discuss the Gold Standard and economic stability.

The gold standard, which links a nation's currency to a certain amount of gold, shaped human behaviour. Because money was backed by a tangible item, it felt stable and secure. The method encouraged saving and financial responsibility.

In the digital age, money is mostly intangible. Digital currencies and electronic transactions have separated money from its physical form, challenging conventional understandings. The shift affects psychology both positively and negatively. One must acknowledge that technology offers convenience. It is crucial to note that this convenience can lead to reckless spending and a disconnect from riches.

This conversation will address the fascinating psychology of scarcity and abundance.

Money has evoked shortage or excess feelings throughout its existence, impacting human behavior. Scarcity can cause hoarding and fear-driven financial decisions. However, abundant resources can lead to overspending and financial complacency. Understanding these psychological responses is crucial to making smart financial decisions.

Since you know about money's evolution, you should realise that it has been a dynamic process that has shaped human behaviour. Money has changed our beliefs, actions, and relationships throughout history. These changes range from barter restrictions to digital currency abstractions. The history of money is essential to understanding its importance in our lives and its complicated psychology, which is fascinating to explore.

3 ii : Cultural and societal influences on money attitudes & Early psychological theories related to money

Individuals' views and behaviours about money are significantly shaped by cultural and socioeconomic variables. These many influences are a reflection of the conventions, values, and economic structures of a particular culture or society. Here, we look at how socioeconomic and cultural factors influence attitudes and practices related to money:

1. Cultural Values and Priorities: Values associated with money are emphasized to varied degrees in various cultures. For instance, providing for the family and storing money for the future are strongly embedded values in various Asian societies.

Individualism and the pursuit of personal success are frequently emphasized in western societies, and this emphasis can present itself in a desire for material wealth.

These cultural norms have an impact on how people prioritize spending, investing, and conserving money.

2. Economic Systems and Social Structures: A society's economic and social systems have a significant impact on people's views about money. For instance, competitiveness and individual financial achievement are frequently emphasised in capitalist society.

Socialism may place a higher value on economic equality and community welfare than on individual wealth.

These systems have the power to influence people's financial behaviours, ambitions, and aspirations.

3. Cultural Rituals and Customs: Cultural customs and rituals pertaining to money can also affect views. Examples include

wedding traditions, in which dowries or presents play a big part in budgeting.

Individuals' financial decisions are influenced by their religious traditions, which frequently involve charitable giving or tithing.

4. Peer and Family Influence: Peer and family networks can shape societal and cultural views toward money. Children's attitudes on money can be significantly influenced by their parents' financial actions and guidance. Similar to peer pressure, social norms within a community can affect how much people spend and save.

5. Social Comparison and Conspicuous Consumption: People have a propensity to participate in social comparison, where they evaluate their own financial situation in relation to that of others.

This analogy may encourage ostentatious consumerism, in which people spend money on outward signs of affluence in an effort to uphold or advance their social status.

To have a thorough understanding of money psychology, one must comprehend these socioeconomic and cultural factors. It draws attention to the variety of monetary attitudes and practices seen in many cultures and social groups and emphasizes the necessity for a nuanced approach to financial education and counseling that takes these contextual considerations into account.

3 iii : EarlyPsychological Theories Related to Money

Psychologists have studied the psychological effects of money throughout history. Although the study of money psychology has developed, the following early theories helped us better understand how money influences our behaviour:

The Theory of Money Neuroses by Sigmund Freud:

The originator of psychoanalysis, Sigmund Freud, studied the idea of "money neuroses." He suggested that deeper psychological conflicts and wants could be the source of people's attitudes and behaviors toward money. For instance, excessive spending may be a symptom of unresolved psychological problems with identity or self-esteem.

Thorstein Veblen's Theory of Conspicuous Consumption: The economist and sociologist Thorstein Veblen is credited with coining the term "conspicuous consumption." He stated that people frequently spend money on goods and services to demonstrate their social standing and success rather than for their actual utility. This idea provided the framework for comprehending how social comparison and status-seeking influence purchasing decisions.

Abraham Maslow's Hierarchy of Needs: Abraham Maslow's well-known hierarchy of needs hypothesis proposed that people place a higher priority on gratifying their fundamental wants than gratifying their more complex demands. In order to meet these requirements, including those for food and shelter as well as self-actualization, money is essential. Understanding where money falls in this hierarchy can help us better understand the psychological factors that influence our judgments towards money.

These early psychological ideas shed important light on the intricate relationship between money and behaviour. These fundamental principles still guide current study and knowledge of how money affects our thoughts, feelings, and actions even though the discipline of money psychology has developed.

Money is a tremendous force that impacts our lives in ways that go beyond basic transactions; it is more than just money. How we manage and interact with our finances is fundamentally influenced by our attitudes and views about money, which are frequently affected by our upbringing, culture, and personal experiences. We'll delve into the intriguing world of monetary attitudes and beliefs in this essay, illuminating their importance and bearing on personal finances.

The Origins of Financial Beliefs:

Our attitudes and thoughts about money frequently develop in childhood. Our early financial conditioning is substantially influenced by our parents, caregivers, and family relationships. For instance, if a youngster grows up in a home that emphasizes saving for the future, they might adopt a favorable mindset toward saving. On the other hand, if kids observe financial difficulties or a lack of financial knowledge, they could grow to have unfavourable or anxious attitudes toward money.

Following are some typical money mindsets:

- Some people have a scarcity mindset, which is the conviction that there is never enough money. They frequently worry about money, which results in a fear-based approach to money management. Their deeply ingrained fear of running out of money frequently affects how much they save and how much they spend.

- Those who have an abundance mindset, on the other hand, see prospects for financial gain and think that resources are abundant. They are more prone to take strategic risks and look for business expansion chances. A attitude of affluence can encourage self-assurance in financial decisions and a readiness to test out novel business opportunities.

- Safety-First Mentality: People that have a safety-first mentality put their financial stability first. They frequently make prudent financial decisions, favouring debt avoidance and low-risk investments. While this way of thinking can offer security, it may also restrict prospects for accumulating wealth.

- You Only Live Once (YOLO) Mindset: The YOLO mindset is characterized by an emphasis on pleasures and gratification that may be had right away. This type of person is more inclined to make impulsive purchases and value short-term pleasure over long-term financial security. Living in the moment can be rewarding, but if it is not balanced with thinking about the future, it can result in financial instability.

Here are some techniques for recognizing and challengingKeeping Money Beliefs in Check:

A critical first step toward financial development and well-being is recognizing and addressing limiting money ideas. This is how:

<u>Self-Awareness</u>: Start by thinking about your personal financial attitudes and

views. What are your views on money? How do these convictions affect your financial choices?

Challenge Your Beliefs: Ask yourself if your money beliefs are serving your financial objectives and general wellbeing. Are they advancing your pursuit of happiness and financial security, or are they impeding you?

Take Financial Education Courses: Learn as much as you can about personal finance. You may be more in control of your finances by having a solid understanding of the basics of budgeting, saving, investing, and debt management.

Seek Advice from a Professional: Think about collaborating with a financial advisor or counsellor who may offer unbiased perspectives and approaches to address any harmful money views or habits.

Beliefs and attitudes about the power of money are more than just theoretical ideas; they have practical effects. They have an impact on how we spend, save, invest, and make financial plans. People can realise their potential for material prosperity and wellbeing by identifying and altering these beliefs.

In conclusion, a key component of personal finance is comprehending the psychology of monetary thoughts and attitudes. These assumptions, which are frequently engrained profoundly, influence our financial decisions and habits. People can take charge of their financial destinies by developing self-awareness and confronting limiting beliefs and making decisions that are consistent with their values, goals, and aspirations. In the end, money is a tool that, depending on the attitudes and beliefs we bring to the table, can either help or hinder us in achieving our goals.

Chapter 4: The role of upbringing and family in shaping money beliefs

Our thoughts, attitudes, and behaviors around money frequently stem from our upbringing and family context. The family is where many of us learn about money. We'll examine how upbringing and family shape our money attitudes in this piece.

1. Early Money Lessons:

Children learn about money through their parents and guardians from a young age. These early lessons can shape their financial outlook.

2. Observational Learning: Children absorb information from their surroundings like sponges. They observe their parents' budgeting, saving,

spending, and investing. They are more inclined to adopt appropriate financial practices if they witness it.

3. Verbal Communication: Parents express their money beliefs verbally. Statements like "money doesn't grow on trees" and "save for a rainy day" promote thrift and financial preparation.

4. Discussing Money as a Taboo Topic: Some families avoid discussing money openly. This silence can make finances mysterious and scary. Children may not grasp their family's finances or how to manage money.

5. Financial Priorities: Parents' financial priorities greatly impact children's money beliefs. A family that values travel and experiences may teach youngsters that spending money on experiences is more important than saving for the future.

6. Family Economic Background: Family economic background might influence money beliefs. Financially strapped families may teach their kids to be frugal

and save. Wealthier families may emphasize investing and wealth-building.

7. Financial Stress: Children may equate money with fear and uncertainty if their family faces financial instability. This might lead to negative money views like that there is never enough money or that financial achievement is elusive.

8. Gender Roles and Money: Families may also instill gender-specific financial values and roles. Traditional gender roles may reinforce the idea that males provide and manage finances while women budget and spend. These positions can shape children's financial perspectives.

9. Inherited Family Money views: Family money views often persist across generations. Children inherit their parents' assets, money values, and attitudes. Breaking inherited money beliefs is difficult but necessary for financial progress.

10. The Influence of Siblings: Siblings can influence money beliefs. The

financial dynamics between siblings might affect money attitudes. If one sibling is the "spender" and another the "saver," these roles might perpetuate money views.

Personal financial progress requires understanding how upbringing and family shape money ideas. It helps people understand their financial habits and make conscious decisions about their money goals. Considering these effects allows people to evaluate if their money beliefs match their financial goals and, if necessary, change them to improve their finances.

4 i : Common money mindsets and their effects

Money mindsets are individuals' deeply ingrained beliefs and attitudes about money. Mindsets have a significant impact on financial behaviors and decisions. This article discusses various money mindsets and how they impact individuals' financial approaches.

- Scarcity mindset is the belief that money and financial resources are limited and there is never enough.

The effects.

-Hoarding is a behavior often associated with individuals who have a scarcity mindset. These individuals tend to save excessively and find it difficult to spend money, even when it is necessary.

-Constant worry about money can lead to stress and anxiety, impacting mental health and overall well-being.

-Focusing on scarcity can result in missed investment opportunities and hesitance to take calculated financial risks.

- The abundance mindset is the belief that there are plenty of opportunities for financial growth and that wealth is achievable.

The effects.

-Having an abundance mindset helps individuals approach financial challenges with optimism and confidence.

-Individuals who are inclined to take risks are more likely to explore various investments and opportunities for creating wealth.

-Having an abundance mindset can increase the likelihood of sharing wealth with others through charitable giving or financial support.

-Financial security and stability are considered crucial, and it is important to steer clear of risks.

- People with a conservative financial mindset tend to make low-risk investments and prioritize saving over spending.

Overemphasizing safety can hinder growth opportunities and wealth accumulation.

Having a peace of mind mindset can bring financial security and reduce stress.

- The YOLO (You Only Live Once) mindset is based on the belief that life is brief and that money should be used for enjoying experiences and pleasures.

-The YOLO mindset leads individuals to prioritize immediate gratification and engage in impulsive spending.

-People who prioritize experiences over material possessions tend to value memorable adventures, but this mindset may not align with long-term financial goals.

-Excessive spending can lead to financial instability and a lack of preparedness for future needs.

Believing in the importance of balancing financial security with enjoying the present and planning for the future.

Having a balanced mindset when it comes to finances involves making strategic choices that consider both saving and investing for the future, as well as enjoying life in the present.

Adaptable individuals are inclined to modify their financial strategies in response to changing circumstances and goals.

Financial wellness is achieved by maintaining a balanced mindset that takes into account both immediate and future financial needs.

- The frugality mindset emphasizes spending money sparingly and minimizing waste.

Frugality mindset helps individuals excel at budgeting and minimizing unnecessary expenses.

Resourcefulness is the ability to find innovative ways to save money, minimize waste, and maximize resources.

Excessive frugality can result in missed opportunities and a lack of enjoyment.

Belief: Material possessions are essential for happiness and status.

The effects.

-Consumerism is a mindset where people prioritize acquiring material goods over other aspects of life.

-Overreliance on material possessions can result in financial strain and debt as people pursue the latest gadgets, cars, or fashion.

Achieving a balanced approach that aligns with your financial goals and values is crucial for long-term financial success and well-being, despite the strengths and weaknesses of each mindset.

Limiting money beliefs can impede financial growth and overall well-being. Attitudes and beliefs about money are often influenced by childhood, society, and past experiences. Challenging and identifying beliefs is important for financial empowerment and success. This article discusses strategies for identifying and overcoming limiting money beliefs.

- Self-reflection is the act of looking inward and examining one's thoughts, feelings, and actions. It involves introspection and self

Start by reflecting on and analyzing your personal beliefs about money. Reflect on your financial attitudes, fears, and behaviors. What are my beliefs about money?

- Beliefs influence financial decisions.

Do my financial decisions reflect recurring patterns influenced by limiting beliefs?

- Pay attention to the thoughts and conversations happening within your mind.

Be mindful of your thoughts and beliefs about money. Do you frequently have negative thoughts about your financial abilities and prospects for wealth? Negative self-perceptions can arise from limiting beliefs. The first step in challenging the validity of something is to acknowledge it.

- Consider reflecting on previous financial experiences that may have influenced your beliefs about money. Did you have a difficult financial upbringing? Have you experienced financial setbacks that made you feel powerless? Understanding the origins of your beliefs can help clarify the reasons behind them.

- Seeking external feedback can help us identify our own limiting beliefs, which can be difficult to recognize on our own. Seeking advice from trusted individuals such as friends, family, or a financial advisor can offer valuable external perspectives. Patterns in your financial behavior that align with limiting beliefs may be pointed out.

- Challenge negative assumptions about limiting money beliefs. Question whether your belief is grounded in facts or assumptions.

Have there been situations that contradict this belief?

Can individuals with diverse beliefs achieve financial success?

- Replace your limiting beliefs with empowering beliefs. Reframe the belief of perpetual financial struggle as the potential for improvement through learning and wise decision-making. Empowering beliefs drive positive financial behavior.
- Financial education is an effective method to challenge limiting beliefs. Learning about budgeting, investing, and personal finance can help individuals gain knowledge and confidence in using evidence-based financial strategies to counter negative beliefs.
- Establishing clear and achievable financial goals is

important. Concrete objectives can help you move away from limiting beliefs and instead focus on taking practical steps towards achieving financial success. Small accomplishments help build confidence and resilience in overcoming challenges.

Visualization is a powerful tool for changing beliefs. Regularly visualize achieving financial goals such as buying a home, paying off debt, or retiring comfortably. Visualization is a helpful tool for fostering a positive mindset and inspiring action.

- Challenging limiting beliefs can be emotionally challenging, but it's important to remember that personal growth is possible for everyone. It is important to celebrate even small successes and understand that change requires time.

- Consider seeking support from financial support groups or professionals such as therapists or financial counselors. Resources are available to help individuals overcome limiting money beliefs by offering structured assistance and a supportive environment.
- Regularly assess your progress in challenging and changing limiting money beliefs. Acknowledge and appreciate your accomplishments while also being open to making necessary changes to your plans. Patience is crucial in this ongoing process.
- Replacing self-imposed barriers with positive beliefs empowers individuals to take control of their financial destiny and work towards achieving their goals and dreams.

4 ii : Money and Emotions

Money's emotional connections are knowing that it's more than a vehicle for transactions and can trigger strong emotions. This emotional connection to money can greatly affect our financial decisions and behaviors. Understanding these relationships helps you make smarter financial decisions.

1. Security and Safety: Money is often associated with security and safety. It comforts and protects against unexpected emergencies. Fear of financial instability can cause anxiety and a desire to save and invest.

2. Social position and Identity: Money can be linked to one's identity and social position. Wealth can signify prosperity or power. Financial setbacks can cause inadequacy or failure.

3. Happiness and Fulfillment: The assumption that money can purchase happiness typically leads to material

items and experiences. People link spending money with happiness, pleasure, and stress relief.

4. Guilt and humiliation: Financial mistakes or perceived mishandling can cause guilt and humiliation. These emotions may cause financial avoidance or concealment.

5. Control and Independence: Money can provide a sense of control over life and decisions. Financial freedom allows people to make decisions that reflect their values and ambitions.

Use these methods for Emotional Spending Management;

Emotional spending occurs when people buy based on feelings rather than finances. Impulsive spending can cause financial hardship and impair long-term aspirations. Strategies for emotional expenditure management:

- Learn what emotions drive your spending. Shopping while worried, bored, depressed, or happy?

- A budget or spending plan should explain your financial goals and priorities. A detailed plan can help you spend more intentionally.
- Practice delaying impulsive purchases. Wait 24 hours or a week before deciding. This delay lets emotions calm and rationality prevail.
- Set clear expenditure limits. For instance, set a monthly non-essential spending limit. Follow these tips to avoid impulsive spending.
- Find non-monetary strategies to manage emotional stress and boredom. Hobbies, exercise, meditation, and friends/therapists can help.
- Share your financial goals and challenges with a trustworthy friend or family member to hold you accountable for spending. Encouragement and reinforcement come from outside.

- Record all expenses, including emotional ones. Reviewing spending habits periodically might reveal patterns and improvement opportunities.
- Set SMART financial goals. Clear goals can motivate and guide expenditure.

Managing money emotions and reducing emotional spending needs self-awareness, discipline, and effort. You may reclaim control of your finances and make decisions that support your long-term financial goals by understanding and using these tactics to your financial emotions.

Chapter 5: The psychology of impulse spending and instant gratification

I had this friend She had always saved her money for a rainy day. Lily became increasingly driven to impulse spending and rapid fulfillment.

The story began one lovely afternoon as Lily passed "blandy Couture." A banner announced a limited-time and stock for that price in the vivid window display of the current fashion trends. Lily approached the store with a surge of excitement, her heart racing. Inside the boutique, sensory overload. Bright colours, soft materials, and tantalising scents filled the air. Lily chose a stunning garment that called to her. She couldn't resist trying it on. She felt instant gratification looking in the mirror. The dress fit flawlessly, and she envisioned all the praises she would get. Lily handed the dress to the clerk and swiped her card without thinking. When the transaction was complete, she was briefly happy. It was like buying the outfit filled a vacuum she didn't know existed. Lily continued her impulse spending for weeks. She felt briefly happy and satisfied after each purchase. The days passed, and her exhilaration was replaced with shame and worry over her funds.

Friends saw Lily's behavior change and raised concern. They invited her to a financial planning class to assist her manage her spending. Lily reluctantly attended.An expert in that class explained impulse spending and rapid reward psychology at the program. Lily discovered that these acts were generally motivated by stress or unpleasant emotions. Shopping helped her cope with life's hardships. Lily realized the entire cost of her impetuous purchases as she listened. The short-lived delight they offered wasn't worth the financial and mental stress. She pledged to improve her habits and restore financial control. Lily overcame her fast gratification cravings with the help of her friends and new information about impulse spending psychology. Though difficult, she began focusing on better stress-reduction methods including exercise, meditation, and family time.

Over time, Lily reduced her impulse buying and rebuilt her savings. She discovered happiness in financial security and mental well-being, not transient things.

Lily passed that store again over the months. The clothing she formerly liked was less enticing. She smiled, knowing she had overcome impulsive spending psychology and achieved contentment.She discovered that knowing impulse spending and quick gratification psychology can help people understand and modify their behaviors.

1. Instant Gratification Trap: The quest for quick benefits or pleasures sometimes comes at the expense of long-term goals or consequences. It's the need to immediately satisfy eating, entertainment, or material desires. It can lead to impulsive expenditure that brings short-term pleasure but subsequent regret.

2. Emotional Triggers: Emotions significantly influence impulse spending. Stress, boredom, despair, or excitement can make people purchase for fast relief. The urgency of these emotions supersedes reasonable thought.

3. The Dopamine Effect: Instant gratification releases dopamine, a neurotransmitter linked to pleasure and reward. Impulsive purchases give your brain a "feel-good" rush of dopamine. This promotes the behavior, making it more likely.

4. Impaired Decision-Making: Instant gratification might hinder decision-making. People often misjudge the long-term effects of their acts in the moment. Their quick gains trump future benefits and financial stability.

5. Consumer Culture and Marketing Tactics: Marketing methods rely on the desire for rapid pleasure. Advertisements and promotions generally emphasize the joy of buying now, increasing haste.

6. The Paradox of Choice: Many options can lead to impulse expenditure. The more possibilities, the harder it is to reject immediate fulfillment. Decision fatigue causes people to make rapid, simple choices.

7. Regret and Emotional Consequences: As quick enjoyment fades, individuals may suffer regret, guilt, or anxiety. They may recognize they overspent or bought impulsively something doesn't fit their values or aspirations.

Managing impulse spending and resisting the allure of instant gratification requires self-awareness and strategic approaches such as:

- Create a budget that allots a certain amount of money for discretionary spending. This controls impulsive purchases and offers a precise framework for making financial decisions.

- Practice putting off satisfaction when you feel the temptation to buy something on a whim. Wait a set amount of time (for instance, 24 hours) before making the choice. Often, during this period, the impulse will fade.

- Determine the feelings or circumstances that lead to impulsive spending. The need for instant gratification can be diminished by discovering healthier coping mechanisms for these feelings, such as through exercise, mindfulness, or creative endeavors.

- Establish definite financial objectives that reflect your values and desires. It may be simpler to reject short-term temptations if you have a sense of purpose and long-term goals.
- Check to see if a purchase fits with your values and financial goals before buying one. Evaluating each purchase's necessity and long-term effects is a key component of mindful spending.
- Limit your exposure to marketing strategies and sales that promote impulsive buying. Limit your time spent on social media and shopping websites, and unsubscribe from commercial emails.
- With a family member or trusted friend who can help you stay responsible for your spending,

discuss your financial issues and aspirations.

- Keep track of every penny you spend, even impulsive purchases. Reviewing your spending patterns can reveal trends and problem areas.

5 i : Financial Stress and Anxiety & Causes and consequences of financial stress

Financial stress and anxiety influence people and families throughout life. Understanding financial stress causes and effects is essential to solving these issues and promoting financial well-being.

Causes of Financial Stress:

- Debt from student loans, credit cards, or mortgages can cause financial stress. Monthly payments and interest might be burdensome.
- Financial strain might result from job loss or a major income drop. People may struggle to pay bills and worry about the future.
- When people don't have enough funds, unexpected medical bills, car repairs, or home upkeep fees can cause stress.

- Lack of Emergency funds: Many people lack emergency funds, making them exposed to financial shocks. A financial safety net gap might increase worry.
- Chronic financial stress can result from living above one's means. Non-essential expenditure can strain finances and cause debt.
- Financial stress can stem from poor financial decisions like overspending or neglecting savings due to financial illiteracy and money management.
  Insurance premiums, copays, and medication costs are rising, which can strain families financially.
- Retirement Concerns: hardship over retirement savings and maintaining one's level of life in old age can cause long-term financial hardship.

The Effects of Financial Stress:
- Financial stress can cause headaches, stomach troubles, and

sleep abnormalities. Chronic stress can cause heart disease.

- Financial stress can cause anxiety, sadness, and other mental health issues. Money worries can damage mental health.
- Personal connections often suffer from financial stress. Money disputes are a primary cause of divorce and strain family and friend ties.
- Decreased Job Performance: Financial worries might lower job performance and limit career advancement.
- Reduced Quality of Life: Financial stress can limit travel, leisure, and personal growth, lowering quality of life.
- Financial stress can affect decision-making, leading to impulsive actions like taking on high-interest debt or liquidating assets.
- Chronic financial stress can make it harder to save, invest, and prepare

for the future, worsening financial problems.

Handling Financial Stress:

- Make a Budget: Create a budget to track income and expenses. This helps uncover ways to cut or reallocate spending to decrease financial stress.
- Create an emergency savings fund to meet unforeseen expenses and provide financial security.
- Seek Financial Advice: A financial expert or counsellor can help you manage debt, save, and invest.
- Systematically reduce and manage debt. Prioritize high-interest debts and consolidate.
- Financial education helps you manage money and make smart decisions.
- Techniques to Reduce Stress: Financial stress can be managed emotionally by mindfulness, meditation, or exercise.

- Complex issues like financial stress and worry can have lifelong impacts. Mitigating these issues and achieving financial stability and well-being requires addressing the core causes and taking proactive steps.

5 ii : Behavioral Economics and Money

Behavioural economics is a branch of economics that explores how psychological and emotional factors influence economic decision-making. It sheds light on why people often deviate from the rational, self-interested behaviour assumed by traditional economic models. When it comes to money, behavioural economics plays a crucial role in understanding why individuals make financial decisions that may not always seem logical from a traditional economic perspective. Here's how behavioural economics intersects with money:

- Behavioural economics acknowledges that individuals have limited cognitive resources and often make decisions under conditions of bounded rationality. In other words, people cannot always process and analyze all available information when making financial choices.

- Behavioural economics identifies various cognitive shortcuts or heuristics that people use when making financial decisions. These can lead to systematic biases and errors in judgement. For example, the availability heuristic makes people give more weight to readily available information, leading to overreaction to recent financial news.

- Prospect theory, developed by Daniel Kahneman and Amos Tversky, is a foundational concept in behavioural economics. It suggests that people evaluate potential financial gains and losses asymmetrically. They often experience greater emotional pain from losses than pleasure from equivalent gains, leading to risk aversion in the domain of loss

- Anchoring is a cognitive bias where people rely heavily on the first piece of information they receive when making financial decisions, even if that information is irrelevant or arbitrary. Subsequent adjustments from this initial anchor are often insufficient, leading to biassed judgments.
- Behavioural economics recognizes that individuals tend to place more value on immediate rewards than on future benefits. This hyperbolic discounting can lead to impulsive spending and inadequate long-term financial planning.
- Mental Accounting:People often categorise money into different mental accounts, such as savings, discretionary spending, and bills. Behavioural economics studies how these mental accounts influence financial decisions and may lead to suboptimal resource allocation.

- Loss aversion refers to the strong preference for avoiding losses over acquiring equivalent gains. This bias can lead to suboptimal financial decisions, such as holding onto losing investments rather than cutting losses.
- Behavioural economics recognizes that social and emotional factors, such as peer pressure, societal norms, and emotional states, play a significant role in financial decisions. These influences can sometimes override rational considerations.
- Behavioural economics promotes the use of "nudges" or changes in the way choices are presented to encourage more desirable financial behaviours. For example, automatic enrollment in retirement savings plans is a nudge that increases participation.
- Behavioural economics can explain phenomena like asset bubbles,

where the prices of assets inflate beyond their intrinsic value due to irrational exuberance and herd behaviour among investors.

Chapter 6: Cognitive biases and their influence on financial decisions & How psychology informs economic policies

Cognitive biases are irrational judgments and decisions. They strongly influence financial decisions, often deviating from conventional economic models. Here are some cognitive biases that affect financial decisions:

- People usually prefer to avoid losses over similar gains. This prejudice may make people unwilling to sell lost investments, even if it's smart.
- Confirmation bias is the tendency to seek out and assess evidence that supports preexisting beliefs. This might lead to overconfidence in investing decisions and contempt for financial opposing views.Many

misrepresent their financial skills. Overconfidence can lead to impulsive trading, unwise investments, and ignoring professional advise.

- Anchoring occurs when people make financial decisions based on the initial information they learn. In compensation discussions, the opening offer often sets the tone.
- Status Quo Bias: People stick to their financial choices even when better ones are offered. This inclination may make retirement savings and investing decisions inert.
- Endowment Effect: People cherish their belongings more because they own them. This may discourage asset sales, even when profitable.
- Herd Behavior: Many investors follow the crowd rather than investigation. Everyone buying or selling based on others' conduct

can cause asset bubbles and market crashes.

- Availability The availability heuristic makes individuals value conveniently accessible information. This may prompt financial markets to overreact to recent events, increasing volatility.

Did you know psychological insights influence economic policymaking? How does psychology affects monetary policy: In "nudging," behavioural economics suggests that legislation and other interventions might gently encourage people to make better choices without limiting their freedom. Automatic retirement savings account enrollment boosts savings growth.

- Consumer Protection: Cognitive biases and behavioral tendencies inform consumer protection laws against predatory lending and deceptive advertising.

- Financial Education: Psychological research informs financial literacy programs to help people recognize cognitive biases and make better financial decisions.
- Behavioral economics informs tax policy that encourage financial activities like retirement savings.
- Social Safety Nets: Welfare and unemployment insurance consider the psychological consequences of financial hardship on households.
- Market regulation: Psychological research helps regulators design regulations and protections that avoid market abuses, excessive speculation, and financial catastrophes.
- Psychological factors affecting investor and consumer confidence are considered by central banks when setting interest rates and monetary policy.
- Behavioral Insights Teams: Some governments employ behavioral

insights teams to incorporate psychological research into decisions and improve government efforts.

Since humans often make irrational decisions, incorporating psychology into economic policy aims to create policies that account for these inclinations, improving economic outcomes and citizen well-being.

6 i : Achieving financial goals, life satisfaction & Balancing material and non-material sources of well-being

Many people value financial objectives because they provide security, independence, and the chance to pursue other goals. Keep these in mind to attain financial objectives and understand how they affect life satisfaction:

- Define, achievable financial goals. Clear goals motivate you to save for retirement, pay off debt, or buy a home.
- Budget your income, expenses, and savings. Setting aside a portion of your salary will help you reach your financial goals.

- Pay off high-interest debt first. Debt reduction will enhance your finances and reduce financial stress, increasing life pleasure.
- Make an emergency reserve for unexpected expenses. A financial safety net eases stress in hard times.
- Learn about investment and diversification to grow your money. You can achieve long-term financial goals via investing.
- Financial counselors and planners can help with money management, especially retirement planning and tax optimization.
- Review your financial goals and progress regularly. To keep on track, adjust your approach.
- Financial objectives often need patience and discipline. Though it takes time, persistence is vital to make substantial progress.

- Be proud of your financial progress. Setting goals boosts motivation and happiness.
- Balancing Happiness from tangible and immaterial sources:
- Financial goals are important, but they should be considered in the context of general well-being, which includes material and intangible fulfillment:
- Financial security, comfortable living conditions, and availability of requirements are all facets of material well-being. Financial goals provide stability and resources for a comfortable life, boosting material well-being.
- Non-material well-being includes emotional, psychological, and social aspects of life. It includes:
- Good Relations Meaningful ties with family and friends enhance life pleasure.
- Happiness depends on physical and mental health.

- Work-Life Balance: Balance between work, personal duties, interests, and leisure is essential for health.
- Personal Growth: Learning, self-fulfillment, and personal growth may improve life satisfaction.To achieve financial goals, it's vital to balance them with non-financial aspects of wellbeing. Focusing on material things may lead to neglecting relationships, health, and personal growth.
- Reflections and Prioritization: Balance material and non-material well-being by considering your values and priorities. Consider how your financial goals suit your values.
- Be alert and grateful to enjoy non-material well-being, which can boost life pleasure.
- Community and Contribution: In addition to financial achievement,

volunteering and helping others might make you happier.

- In the end, financial goals are important, but it's also important to comprehend the holistic nature of wellbeing and find a balance between material and non-material enjoyment and fulfillment.

6 ii : investing and Risk Perception, Behavioural aspects of investing, Risk tolerance and decision-making in investment & Overcoming common investment biases

Investing is a critical financial activity that involves allocating resources to various assets with the expectation of generating returns. The field of behavioural economics sheds light on the psychological factors that influence investment decisions, including risk perception, risk tolerance, and cognitive biases. Here's an overview of these aspects and how they relate to investing:

A. Behavioral Aspects of Investing:

1. Loss Aversion: Investors often feel the pain of losses more acutely

than the pleasure of gains, leading to risk-averse behavior. They may sell investments prematurely to avoid losses, missing out on potential gains.

2. Overconfidence: Overconfidence bias can lead investors to believe they have superior knowledge or predictive abilities. This can result in excessive trading and taking on higher risks than they can handle.

3. Herding Behavior: Investors tend to follow the crowd, especially during market booms or crashes. This herd mentality can contribute to bubbles and market volatility.

4. Confirmation Bias: Investors may seek out information that confirms their existing beliefs about investments and ignore contradictory information, leading to biased decision-making.

5. Anchoring: Anchoring occurs when investors fixate on a specific price or information point and

base their decisions on that
anchor.

B. Risk Tolerance and Decision-Making in Investment:

1. Tolerating risk Tolerance: tolerance refers to your individual ability and to take financial risk. It varies from person to person and can depend on factors like age, financial goals, and personal circumstances.
2. Asset Allocation: Determining the appropriate mix of assets (e.g., stocks, bonds, real estate) in an investment portfolio is influenced by risk tolerance. Risk-averse individuals may prefer a more conservative allocation with lower potential returns but less risk, while risk-tolerant individuals may opt for a more aggressive allocation.

3. Time Horizon: Risk tolerance is closely tied to the investment time horizon. Longer time horizons allow for greater tolerance of market fluctuations and the potential for recovery from losses.
4. Diversification: Diversifying a portfolio across different asset classes can help manage risk. Investors with lower risk tolerance may opt for broader diversification to reduce exposure to any single asset's volatility.

C. Overcoming Common Investment Biases:

1. Education: Increasing financial literacy and understanding of investment principles can help investors recognize and overcome cognitive biases. Knowledgeable investors are better equipped to make rational decisions.

2. Objective Assessment: Seek objective advice from financial professionals who can provide an unbiased perspective on investment choices.
3. Investment Plan: Develop a well-defined investment plan that outlines your financial goals, risk tolerance, and asset allocation strategy.
4. Dollar-Cost Averaging: Instead of trying to time the market, consider a dollar-cost averaging strategy. This involves investing a fixed amount regularly, which can reduce the impact of market volatility on your portfolio.
5. Emotional Control: Practise emotional control by not letting fear or greed drive investment decisions. Set clear rules for buying and selling investments based on your plan rather than reacting to short-term market fluctuations.

6. Professional Advice: If you find it challenging to overcome biases and manage investments effectively, consider working with a financial advisor who can provide guidance and objective recommendations.

Understanding the behavioral aspects of investing, assessing your risk tolerance, and actively addressing cognitive biases can lead to more informed and successful investment decisions, ultimately helping you work towards your financial goals.

Chapter 7 : The Future of Money Psychology

Money psychology, which studies how human behaviour affects financial decisions, is poised for a fascinating shift. As we look ahead, this field will revolutionise how we view, interact with, and manage our finances. This essay explores hopeful trends and breakthroughs that could shape money psychology's future.

Digital Transformation and Behavioral Finance:

Financial management has been forever changed by the digital revolution. From internet banking to smartphone payment apps, technology has streamlined our finances. This digital upheaval will continue to change our money psyche.The biggest change we can expect is data-driven decision-making. Artificial intelligence-powered data analytics will enable financial institutions and fintech startups to collect and analyse massive volumes of financial data. This data will underpin personalised financial advice and insights, driving educated financial decision-making. These insights will help people make financial decisions that match their values and ambitions.

Behavioural finance apps will also change how we view and use money. These apps will be our own financial psychologists, employing behavioral economics to guide us to good financial behaviors. Gamification, behavioral nudges, and personalised feedback may help us save more, invest wisely, and make long-term financial decisions.

Digital assets will change money psychology as Bitcoin and Ethereum gain popularity and central banks globally develop central bank digital currencies (CBDCs). Understanding how psychological aspects like volatility, speculative ness, and decentralization affect our perception of digital currencies will become increasingly important.

Behavioral Economics and Policy Design:

The integration of behavioural economics into policymaking will grow. Governments and regulators will use behavioural insights to create ethical financial rules.

Financial well-being "nudging" is an example of this tendency. Nudges will continue to encourage saving, investing, and retirement planning by governments. Automatic enrollment in retirement plans, tax incentives for savings, or bill payment reminders are examples of nudges. Policymakers can gently lead people toward long-term financial goals using behavioural science.

Before implementing new financial regulations, behavioural effect studies will be developed. These assessments will examine how suggested policies affect consumer behaviour and well-being. To guarantee that policies achieve their economic goals and consider the psychological and behavioural effects on individuals and society,

Finance Education and Empowerment:

The future of money psychology emphasises financial empowerment and education. Here, too, hopeful trends promise to equip people with the knowledge and skills to make smart financial decisions.

One trend is personalised financial education. Financial education platforms and tools will tailor financial education to individual knowledge gaps and financial goals. Financial education will now be customised to each person's needs.

Gamification will also be used to make financial education fun. Interactive games and simulations will help people practise financial decisions in a risk-free environment and gain the confidence to handle real-world financial difficulties.

Mental and financial health:

Future research will focus on mental health and money psychology. Financial well-being is linked to emotional and psychological health.

Financial stress and anxiety may be addressed through mental health and financial counselling from financial institutions and businesses. These services will acknowledge that financial and emotional well-being are strongly related and that fixing one can dramatically affect the other.

Also, financial planning and advisory services will increasingly use well-being criteria. These measures will regard an individual's emotional and psychological health as important to their financial performance beyond income and savings. Recognizing that our financial and emotional lives are interconnected will change how we approach money and well-being.

Ethical and Sustainable Investment:

Future money psychology will interact with ethical and sustainable investing, which is fascinating. As individuals and institutions prioritize investments that match with their values and benefit society and the environment, the psychology of these choices will be studied.

Impact investors—those who seek financial rewards and social or environmental benefits—will be studied. Understanding why people invest in impact and how they make decisions can help connect financial interests with societal aims.

Additionally, the field will study behavioural biases that affect sustainable consumption and investment. We'll analyse why people hesitate to make eco-friendly financial decisions, even when the evidence supports them. Understanding these biases allows us to promote eco-conscious financial decisions and create a more sustainable financial landscape.

Digital Identity and Financial Trust: As digital identity systems become increasingly common, money psychology must adjust to digital trust concepts. Trust is essential to financial transactions, thus studying how people create and retain trust in digital financial interactions is crucial.

Data security, identity verification, and user experience will shape digital transaction confidence. Research will examine psychological aspects that affect digital financial platform trustworthiness, leading to better secure and user-friendly systems.

In the future, AI-powered financial advisors will be more sophisticated than ever before. AI systems will give tailored, emotionally intelligent financial advice, transforming financial advice.

Advanced AI will recognize and address users' emotional and financial issues through natural language processing and sentiment analysis. Financial aid seekers will receive 24/7 assistance from these AI-powered counsellors.

In conclusion, money psychology will continue to study how human behaviour affects financial decisions. Technological advances, behavioural insights, and comprehensive financial well-being define the future. As these developments continue, people and societies will negotiate money's complexity with confidence and resilience. Financial decisions will soon be about people and their particular objectives, values, and well-being. Money psychology will guide this financial empowerment and fulfilment path.

Business and investment decisions involve ambition, caution, opportunity, and risk. One must be aware of and able to assess hazards to navigate this difficult terrain. In this essay, we will discuss risk evaluation in business and investing environments, decision-making, decisive action, and staying positive in the face of adversity.

Understanding Business and Investment Risks:

Business ventures and investments are risky. These risks include financial, operational, market, and strategic. In business, starting a new company, entering new markets, or releasing a new product all have risks. Investments in stocks, bonds, real estate, or a new business subject one to financial market swings, economic downturns, and unexpected events.

The Risk Assessment Process:

Identification: Identification is the initial stage in risk assessment. Entrepreneurs and investors must identify hazards systematically. This may comprise risk assessments, market research, and scenario preparation.

Assessment: Assess hazards' impact and likelihood after identification. This entails probabilizing risk events and calculating their effects.

After identifying risks, firms and investors should design risk mitigation methods. Diversification, hedging, insurance, and emergency planning are examples.

Decision-Making: The decision-making process includes risk assessment. It helps balance rewards and dangers. A calculated risk-reward ratio guides decisions.

Making a Decision:

Business and investing success depends on decisive action. After assessing risks and making decisions, act. Committing to a course and applying risk mitigation methods is decisive action.

Execution: A well-planned company plan must be executed precisely. Effective resource allocation, progress tracking, and strategy adjustments are required. Trading, managing a diverse portfolio, and staying the course amid market swings are investments.

Decisive action requires flexibility. Business planning and investment strategies may need to be adjusted due to unexpected circumstances. Success requires resilience and adaptation.

Continuous monitoring and learning are essential after action. Businesses and investors should assess financial performance and market circumstances regularly. Improving decision-making requires learning from triumphs and failures.

Positive Thinking Power:

Maintaining a positive outlook during risks and failures is sometimes overlooked but crucial. A positive mindset is confronting obstacles with positivity and resilience, not ignoring dangers or setbacks.

Confidence and optimism: A positive outlook gives business executives and investors confidence to overcome challenges. It helps retain a long-term perspective despite short-term disappointments.

Positive thinking increases risk tolerance. Positive people see dangers as opportunities, which can lead to inventive solutions and competitive benefits.

Stress reduction: Positivity reduces business and investment stress. Clear decision-making and well-being require stress management.

Learning and Growth: A cheerful outlook promotes growth. Instead of concentrating on setbacks, optimistic people learn from them.

Finally, assessing business and investment risks is vital to make educated decisions. It involves risk identification, assessment, and mitigation, which are crucial to decision-making. Taking decisive action is also important since it implements decisions and enables for growth. A cheerful outlook can also make the difference between overcoming adversity. It helps people manage the intricacies of business and investment with endurance, inventiveness, and unrelenting resolve, leading to greater success and fulfilment.

7 i : Saving

Saving money involves the distinction between your income and your cravings for material possessions. This financial practice grants you a versatile edge in multiple facets of your life and bestows upon you an immeasurable sense of tranquility. It empowers you with the freedom to make decisions aligned with your wishes and necessities, thus affording you the capacity to navigate life's twists and turns with confidence.

Did you know???

The United States stock market has historically delivered a consistent 6.8% return after adjusting for inflation. To emphasize, this figure is 6.8%.

For decades, our American capitalist system has generated an average return of 6.8% after factoring in an average inflation rate of 3.1% (resulting in a total return of 9.9%). This is a manifestation of the law of averages, a potent force that can work in our favor if we understand how to leverage it and if we are content with achieving average returns. It's worth noting that research has repeatedly shown that many investors fall short of even achieving these average returns. The ultimate objective is to consistently earn the average return over an extended period. Why? There are two compelling reasons:

1. A 6.8% return above and beyond inflation is a commendable rate of return.
2. Pursuing average returns serves to shield our emotions from the extreme market fluctuations (volatility) that might otherwise trigger panic and impulsive decisions to exit the market.

Conclusion

Instead of trying to time the market, you might want to use a technique like dollar-cost averaging. It's important to know that 85% of large-cap fund managers didn't do better than the S&P 500. Even though there are some good reasons to pick stocks, you should be aware that the odds of constantly succeeding at this are not in your favor. So, it's best to put most of your money into low-cost index funds.

It's important to keep an eye out for greed's sneaky ways. Don't fall into the mental mistake of trying to keep up with other people, which is often called "keeping up with the Joneses." Instead of giving in to peer pressure, focus on staying on a reasonable financial path.

It is very important to invest a lot when you are younger. Warren Buffett is a good example of someone who made a lot of money because he started investing early on instead of counting only on getting very high returns. The amazing power of compounding shows how smart it is to start saving early for your financial future.

Also, it's important to note that building wealth often depends more on how much you save than on how much money you make or how much you get back from investing. Putting away a regular amount of your pay can be a powerful way to build wealth over time.

Also, it's totally fine to put peace of mind ahead of always trying to get the most out of your money. For example, let's say you have college loans with an interest rate of 4%. Paying off these loans instead of spending elsewhere, even if it could bring in a higher return, is a smart choice that will give you peace of mind about your finances.

Also, it's best to be ready for the unexpected on the stock market and fight the urge to pull out money when the market goes down. Keeping a smart 1/3 gap can be a good way to go. For example, if the average return on the Indian stock market in the past, after taking inflation into account, was 6.9%, it would be smart to plan for a safer 4.6%. This is especially important because you could leave during a bear market, and past trends don't always happen again.

When it comes to timing the market, it's important to know that only 9% of tactical mutual funds that try to change the stock-to-bond ratio based on economic predictions have regularly done better than a passive investment strategy. Compounding means that you have to go through market downturns, which is a price worth paying for long-term financial success. Think of market volatility as the price you pay for the chance to make money by trading.

Lastly, keep in mind that people, especially those in the media, tend to be pessimistic, even though history shows that things tend to get better over time. Keeping an eye on the long term can help you keep a steady hand in the often-volatile world of finance.

My *Daily*

BUSINESS

PLANNER

S M T W T F S

MY SCHEDULE
FOR TODAY

6 am	
7 am	
8 am	
9 am	
10 am	
11 am	
12 am	
1 pm	
2 pm	
3 pm	
4 pm	
5 pm	
6 pm	
7 pm	
8 pm	
9 pm	
10 pm	

MY PRIORITIES TODAY

NOTES

GOALS

- ☐ _____
- ☐ _____
- ☐ _____
- ☐ _____
- ☐ _____
- ☐ _____
- ☐ _____

My Daily

BUSINESS

PLANNER

DATE

(S) (M) (T) (W) (T) (F) (S)

MY SCHEDULE
FOR TODAY

6 am	
7 am	
8 am	
9 am	
10 am	
11 am	
12 am	
1 pm	
2 pm	
3 pm	
4 pm	
5 pm	
6 pm	
7 pm	
8 pm	
9 pm	
10 pm	

MY PRIORITIES
TODAY

NOTES

GOALS

☐
☐
☐
☐
☐
☐
☐

My Daily

BUSINESS
PLANNER

DATE _____

(S) (M) (T) (W) (T) (F) (S)

MY SCHEDULE
FOR TODAY

6 am	
7 am	
8 am	
9 am	
10 am	
11 am	
12 am	
1 pm	
2 pm	
3 pm	
4 pm	
5 pm	
6 pm	
7 pm	
8 pm	
9 pm	
10 pm	

MY PRIORITIES TODAY

NOTES

GOALS

- ☐ _____
- ☐ _____
- ☐ _____
- ☐ _____
- ☐ _____
- ☐ _____
- ☐ _____

139

My Daily

BUSINESS

PLANNER

DATE

S M T W T F S

MY SCHEDULE FOR TODAY

6 am	
7 am	
8 am	
9 am	
10 am	
11 am	
12 am	
1 pm	
2 pm	
3 pm	
4 pm	
5 pm	
6 pm	
7 pm	
8 pm	
9 pm	
10 pm	

MY PRIORITIES TODAY

NOTES

GOALS

- ☐
- ☐
- ☐
- ☐
- ☐
- ☐
- ☐

My *Daily*

BUSINESS

PLANNER

S M T W T F S

MY SCHEDULE
FOR TODAY

6 am	
7 am	
8 am	
9 am	
10 am	
11 am	
12 am	
1 pm	
2 pm	
3 pm	
4 pm	
5 pm	
6 pm	
7 pm	
8 pm	
9 pm	
10 pm	

MY PRIORITIES TODAY

NOTES

GOALS

- ☐ _____
- ☐ _____
- ☐ _____
- ☐ _____
- ☐ _____
- ☐ _____
- ☐ _____

141

My *Daily*

B U S I N E S S
P L A N N E R

(S) (M) (T) (W) (T) (F) (S)

MY SCHEDULE
FOR TODAY

6 am	
7 am	
8 am	
9 am	
10 am	
11 am	
12 am	
1 pm	
2 pm	
3 pm	
4 pm	
5 pm	
6 pm	
7 pm	
8 pm	
9 pm	
10 pm	

MY PRIORITIES
TODAY

NOTES

GOALS

- ☐ ....
- ☐ ....
- ☐ ....
- ☐ ....
- ☐ ....
- ☐ ....
- ☐ ....

142

My Daily

BUSINESS

PLANNER

DATE

S M T W T F S

MY SCHEDULE
FOR TODAY

6 am	
7 am	
8 am	
9 am	
10 am	
11 am	
12 am	
1 pm	
2 pm	
3 pm	
4 pm	
5 pm	
6 pm	
7 pm	
8 pm	
9 pm	
10 pm	

MY PRIORITIES
TODAY

NOTES

GOALS

- ☐ _____
- ☐ _____
- ☐ _____
- ☐ _____
- ☐ _____
- ☐ _____
- ☐ _____
- ☐ _____

143

My Daily

BUSINESS

PLANNER

DATE

S M T W T F S

MY SCHEDULE FOR TODAY

6 am	
7 am	
8 am	
9 am	
10 am	
11 am	
12 am	
1 pm	
2 pm	
3 pm	
4 pm	
5 pm	
6 pm	
7 pm	
8 pm	
9 pm	
10 pm	

MY PRIORITIES TODAY

NOTES

GOALS

- [ ]
- [ ]
- [ ]
- [ ]
- [ ]
- [ ]
- [ ]

My *Daily*

B U S I N E S S
P L A N N E R

DATE ....

(S) (M) (T) (W) (T) (F) (S)

MY SCHEDULE FOR TODAY

6 am	
7 am	
8 am	
9 am	
10 am	
11 am	
12 am	
1 pm	
2 pm	
3 pm	
4 pm	
5 pm	
6 pm	
7 pm	
8 pm	
9 pm	
10 pm	

MY PRIORITIES TODAY

NOTES

GOALS

- ☐ _____
- ☐ _____
- ☐ _____
- ☐ _____
- ☐ _____
- ☐ _____
- ☐ _____

My *Daily*

BUSINESS
PLANNER

DATE _____

S M T W T F S

MY SCHEDULE FOR TODAY

6 am	
7 am	
8 am	
9 am	
10 am	
11 am	
12 am	
1 pm	
2 pm	
3 pm	
4 pm	
5 pm	
6 pm	
7 pm	
8 pm	
9 pm	
10 pm	

MY PRIORITIES TODAY

NOTES

GOALS

- ☐ _____
- ☐ _____
- ☐ _____
- ☐ _____
- ☐ _____
- ☐ _____
- ☐ _____

146

My Daily

B U S I N E S S
P L A N N E R

DATE

S M T W T F S

MY SCHEDULE
FOR TODAY

6 am	
7 am	
8 am	
9 am	
10 am	
11 am	
12 am	
1 pm	
2 pm	
3 pm	
4 pm	
5 pm	
6 pm	
7 pm	
8 pm	
9 pm	
10 pm	

MY PRIORITIES
TODAY

NOTES

GOALS

- ☐ _____
- ☐ _____
- ☐ _____
- ☐ _____
- ☐ _____
- ☐ _____
- ☐ _____

My *Daily*

BUSINESS
PLANNER

DATE ....

S M T W T F S

MY SCHEDULE FOR TODAY

6 am	
7 am	
8 am	
9 am	
10 am	
11 am	
12 am	
1 pm	
2 pm	
3 pm	
4 pm	
5 pm	
6 pm	
7 pm	
8 pm	
9 pm	
10 pm	

MY PRIORITIES TODAY

NOTES

GOALS

☐ ....
☐ ....
☐ ....
☐ ....
☐ ....
☐ ....
☐ ....

My *Daily*

BUSINESS
PLANNER

DATE _____

(S) (M) (T) (W) (T) (F) (S)

MY SCHEDULE
FOR TODAY

6 am	
7 am	
8 am	
9 am	
10 am	
11 am	
12 am	
1 pm	
2 pm	
3 pm	
4 pm	
5 pm	
6 pm	
7 pm	
8 pm	
9 pm	
10 pm	

MY PRIORITIES TODAY

NOTES

GOALS

☐ ....
☐ ....
☐ ....
☐ ....
☐ ....
☐ ....
☐ ....

149

My *Daily*

BUSINESS

PLANNER

S M T W T F S

**MY SCHEDULE
FOR TODAY**

6 am	
7 am	
8 am	
9 am	
10 am	
11 am	
12 am	
1 pm	
2 pm	
3 pm	
4 pm	
5 pm	
6 pm	
7 pm	
8 pm	
9 pm	
10 pm	

**MY PRIORITIES
TODAY**

NOTES

GOALS

- [ ]
- [ ]
- [ ]
- [ ]
- [ ]
- [ ]
- [ ]

150

My *Daily*

B U S I N E S S

P L A N N E R

S M T W T F S

MY SCHEDULE
FOR TODAY

6 am	
7 am	
8 am	
9 am	
10 am	
11 am	
12 am	
1 pm	
2 pm	
3 pm	
4 pm	
5 pm	
6 pm	
7 pm	
8 pm	
9 pm	
10 pm	

GOALS

- [ ]
- [ ]
- [ ]
- [ ]
- [ ]
- [ ]
- [ ]

MY PRIORITIES TODAY

NOTES

My Daily

BUSINESS

PLANNER

S M T W T F S

MY SCHEDULE FOR TODAY

6 am	
7 am	
8 am	
9 am	
10 am	
11 am	
12 am	
1 pm	
2 pm	
3 pm	
4 pm	
5 pm	
6 pm	
7 pm	
8 pm	
9 pm	
10 pm	

MY PRIORITIES TODAY

NOTES

GOALS

- [ ]
- [ ]
- [ ]
- [ ]
- [ ]
- [ ]
- [ ]

152

My Daily
BUSINESS
PLANNER

DATE

S M T W T F S

MY SCHEDULE FOR TODAY

6 am	
7 am	
8 am	
9 am	
10 am	
11 am	
12 am	
1 pm	
2 pm	
3 pm	
4 pm	
5 pm	
6 pm	
7 pm	
8 pm	
9 pm	
10 pm	

MY PRIORITIES TODAY

NOTES

GOALS

- [ ]
- [ ]
- [ ]
- [ ]
- [ ]
- [ ]
- [ ]

153

My *Daily*

BUSINESS

PLANNER

DATE ....

Ⓢ Ⓜ Ⓣ Ⓦ Ⓣ Ⓕ Ⓢ

MY SCHEDULE FOR TODAY

6 am	
7 am	
8 am	
9 am	
10 am	
11 am	
12 am	
1 pm	
2 pm	
3 pm	
4 pm	
5 pm	
6 pm	
7 pm	
8 pm	
9 pm	
10 pm	

MY PRIORITIES TODAY

NOTES

GOALS

☐ ....
☐ ....
☐ ....
☐ ....
☐ ....
☐ ....
☐ ....

154

My *Daily*

BUSINESS
PLANNER

S M T W T F S

MY SCHEDULE
FOR TODAY

6 am	
7 am	
8 am	
9 am	
10 am	
11 am	
12 am	
1 pm	
2 pm	
3 pm	
4 pm	
5 pm	
6 pm	
7 pm	
8 pm	
9 pm	
10 pm	

MY PRIORITIES
TODAY

NOTES

GOALS

- [ ]
- [ ]
- [ ]
- [ ]
- [ ]
- [ ]
- [ ]

My *Daily*

BUSINESS

PLANNER

S M T W T F S

MY SCHEDULE
FOR TODAY

6 am	
7 am	
8 am	
9 am	
10 am	
11 am	
12 am	
1 pm	
2 pm	
3 pm	
4 pm	
5 pm	
6 pm	
7 pm	
8 pm	
9 pm	
10 pm	

MY PRIORITIES TODAY

NOTES

GOALS

- [ ]
- [ ]
- [ ]
- [ ]
- [ ]
- [ ]
- [ ]

156

My *Daily*

B U S I N E S S

P L A N N E R

S M T W T F S

MY SCHEDULE
FOR TODAY

6 am	
7 am	
8 am	
9 am	
10 am	
11 am	
12 am	
1 pm	
2 pm	
3 pm	
4 pm	
5 pm	
6 pm	
7 pm	
8 pm	
9 pm	
10 pm	

MY PRIORITIES TODAY

NOTES

GOALS

- [ ] _____
- [ ] _____
- [ ] _____
- [ ] _____
- [ ] _____
- [ ] _____
- [ ] _____

My Daily

BUSINESS

PLANNER

DATE

S M T W T F S

MY SCHEDULE
FOR TODAY

6 am	
7 am	
8 am	
9 am	
10 am	
11 am	
12 am	
1 pm	
2 pm	
3 pm	
4 pm	
5 pm	
6 pm	
7 pm	
8 pm	
9 pm	
10 pm	

MY PRIORITIES
TODAY

NOTES

GOALS

- [ ]
- [ ]
- [ ]
- [ ]
- [ ]
- [ ]
- [ ]

My Daily

BUSINESS
PLANNER

DATE ....

S M T W T F S

MY SCHEDULE FOR TODAY

6 am	
7 am	
8 am	
9 am	
10 am	
11 am	
12 am	
1 pm	
2 pm	
3 pm	
4 pm	
5 pm	
6 pm	
7 pm	
8 pm	
9 pm	
10 pm	

MY PRIORITIES TODAY

NOTES

GOALS

- [ ] ....
- [ ] ....
- [ ] ....
- [ ] ....
- [ ] ....
- [ ] ....
- [ ] ....

My Daily

BUSINESS

PLANNER

S M T W T F S

MY SCHEDULE
FOR TODAY

6 am	
7 am	
8 am	
9 am	
10 am	
11 am	
12 am	
1 pm	
2 pm	
3 pm	
4 pm	
5 pm	
6 pm	
7 pm	
8 pm	
9 pm	
10 pm	

MY PRIORITIES TODAY

NOTES

GOALS

- ☐ _____
- ☐ _____
- ☐ _____
- ☐ _____
- ☐ _____
- ☐ _____
- ☐ _____

My Daily

BUSINESS

PLANNER

(S) (M) (T) (W) (T) (F) (S)

MY SCHEDULE
FOR TODAY

6 am	
7 am	
8 am	
9 am	
10 am	
11 am	
12 am	
1 pm	
2 pm	
3 pm	
4 pm	
5 pm	
6 pm	
7 pm	
8 pm	
9 pm	
10 pm	

MY PRIORITIES TODAY

NOTES

GOALS

- ☐
- ☐
- ☐
- ☐
- ☐
- ☐
- ☐

My Daily

BUSINESS

PLANNER

S M T W T F S

MY SCHEDULE
FOR TODAY

6 am	
7 am	
8 am	
9 am	
10 am	
11 am	
12 am	
1 pm	
2 pm	
3 pm	
4 pm	
5 pm	
6 pm	
7 pm	
8 pm	
9 pm	
10 pm	

MY PRIORITIES
TODAY

NOTES

GOALS

- [ ]
- [ ]
- [ ]
- [ ]
- [ ]
- [ ]
- [ ]

My *Daily*

BUSINESS

PLANNER

(S) (M) (T) (W) (T) (F) (S)

MY SCHEDULE
FOR TODAY

6 am	
7 am	
8 am	
9 am	
10 am	
11 am	
12 am	
1 pm	
2 pm	
3 pm	
4 pm	
5 pm	
6 pm	
7 pm	
8 pm	
9 pm	
10 pm	

MY PRIORITIES TODAY

NOTES

GOALS

- [ ] _____
- [ ] _____
- [ ] _____
- [ ] _____
- [ ] _____
- [ ] _____
- [ ] _____

My *Daily*

B U S I N E S S
P L A N N E R

DATE ....

S M T W T F S

MY SCHEDULE FOR TODAY

6 am	
7 am	
8 am	
9 am	
10 am	
11 am	
12 am	
1 pm	
2 pm	
3 pm	
4 pm	
5 pm	
6 pm	
7 pm	
8 pm	
9 pm	
10 pm	

MY PRIORITIES TODAY

NOTES

GOALS

- ☐ ....
- ☐ ....
- ☐ ....
- ☐ ....
- ☐ ....
- ☐ ....
- ☐ ....

My Daily

BUSINESS

PLANNER

DATE ....

S M T W T F S

MY SCHEDULE
FOR TODAY

6 am	
7 am	
8 am	
9 am	
10 am	
11 am	
12 am	
1 pm	
2 pm	
3 pm	
4 pm	
5 pm	
6 pm	
7 pm	
8 pm	
9 pm	
10 pm	

MY PRIORITIES TODAY

NOTES

GOALS

- [ ] ....
- [ ] ....
- [ ] ....
- [ ] ....
- [ ] ....
- [ ] ....
- [ ] ....

My *Daily*

BUSINESS
PLANNER

DATE _____

S M T W T F S

MY SCHEDULE FOR TODAY

6 am	
7 am	
8 am	
9 am	
10 am	
11 am	
12 am	
1 pm	
2 pm	
3 pm	
4 pm	
5 pm	
6 pm	
7 pm	
8 pm	
9 pm	
10 pm	

MY PRIORITIES TODAY

NOTES

GOALS

- [ ] _____
- [ ] _____
- [ ] _____
- [ ] _____
- [ ] _____
- [ ] _____
- [ ] _____

166